T0090146

Praise for

THE MOTHER KNOT

"Harrison's nuanced and sure-handed prose carries the day. . . . The ritualistic expiation of what seems to be her own rage feels emotionally right and, in the end, very brave."
—*The Washington Post Book World*

"[A] brief, poetic meditation on the exorcism of family pain."
—*Publishers Weekly*

"In prose that manages to be both luminous and economical, in sentences that feel as effortless as breathing, Kathryn Harrison poignantly details the lengths to which one daughter must go, in order to finally let go."
—HOPE EDELMAN, author of *Motherless Daughters*

"*The Mother Knot* is a prose poem dedicated to performing a difficult task at which Kathryn Harrison always elegantly succeeds. Here, once again, she has found great beauty in limning hard truths. She is one of the most compelling writers I know, a true artist whose formidable talent is matched by her courage."
—ELIZABETH BERG, author of *The Year of Pleasures*

"Kathryn Harrison's new memoir, written with razor blades and honey, is a compelling mother-daughter study, full of truths about our lives. The book is moving and beautifully written."
—ERICA JONG, author of *Sappho's Leap*

ALSO BY KATHRYN HARRISON

THE MOTHER KNOT

THE MOTHER KNOT

A Memoir

Kathryn Harrison

RANDOM HOUSE
TRADE PAPERBACKS
NEW YORK

2005 Random House Trade Paperback Edition

Copyright © 2004 by Kathryn Harrison

Published in the United States by Random House Trade Paperbacks,
an imprint of The Random House Publishing Group, a division of
Random House, Inc., New York.

RANDOM HOUSE TRADE PAPERBACKS and colophon are trademarks
of Random House, Inc.

Originally published in hardcover in the United States by Random House,
an imprint of The Random House Publishing Group, a division of
Random House, Inc., in 2004.

Library of Congress Cataloging-in-Publication Data

Harrison, Kathryn.
The Mother Knot / Kathryn Harrison.
p.   cm.
ISBN 978-0-8129-7150-7
1. Harrison, Kathryn—Mental health.   2. Depression, Mental—Patients—
United States—Biography.   3. Anorexia—Patients—United States—Biography.
4. Affective disorders—Patients—United States—Biography.   I. Title.
RC537.H348 2004
362.196′8527′0092—dc22   [B]   2003061769

www.atrandom.com

Book design by Carole Lowenstein

146119709

For Janet

Your vision will become clear
only when you can look into
your own heart.
Who looks outside, dreams;
who looks inside, awakes.
—CARL JUNG

THE MOTHER KNOT

THERE'S still a bottle of milk in our freezer, six ounces expressed from my breasts and poured into a sterilized container to have on hand should our daughter get hungry when I'm not home. There used to be more frozen bottles, as many as a dozen, but our daughter is three now; she hasn't nursed for almost a year. The single bottle hidden among the foil-wrapped leftovers and cartons of ice cream is one I saved for myself—a benign little keepsake, or so I thought at the time, unable to imagine that the apparently sentimental souvenir would be revealed as a dark, even perverse, fetish.

The daughter for whom I froze my milk is our third child. After she was born I had a tubal ligation. I nursed her longer than I did her older sister and brother because I knew I wouldn't be returning to this one thing I did so well, so happily. Never again, under any other circumstances, would I be able to answer a loved one's

desire so completely. My daughter passed one after another milestone of babyhood—she walked, talked, used
her full set of teeth to eat whatever she wanted—and
still I postponed the separation of weaning.

By May 2002 my youngest child was twenty-six
months old and lifted my shirt only at bedtime or when
she needed reassurance, comfort that was hers whether
she nursed or not. At the end of that month I used a
business trip to help me accomplish what I'd avoided as
long as I was near her. All day and all night for a week I
wore a tight sports bra, the effect of which was to bind
my aching breasts and suppress the production of milk.
When I showered my chest throbbed and my nipples
leaked. For a few days they did. Then the body began
to understand; the swelling diminished.

Back home, despite a sudden June heat wave, I
wore high-necked shirts and tucked them into my
waistband. When my daughter asked to nurse, fondling
me through the fabric, I told her how proud I was to
have such a wonderful big girl, and together we listed
the differences between big girls and babies, who drink
from their mothers and can't have apple juice or chocolate milk in a cup. A secure and cheerful child, my
daughter adapted quickly. I, however, suffered a plunge

in mood and waited for what didn't happen: to feel better, or at least less bereft.

Summer became a season of compulsive work and little else. Diversions I'd enjoyed in the past—trips to the beach, dinner parties, movies, tennis—were leached of pleasure, colorless, tedious, exhausting. Everything required more energy than I had, especially pretending that I wasn't depressed. Sleep was elusive, and I began, on those nights I was awake hours after turning off the light, to sneak a half milligram of stale Xanax.

The tranquilizer had been prescribed four years earlier, when I'd suffered a depression serious enough that, once hospitalized, I found a metal mirror in my bathroom, not a glass one I could break and use against myself. The admitting nurse searched my overnight bag and confiscated my disposable razor; she told me that there were no circumstances under which I was permitted to close my door and that if I wanted to shave my legs or armpits I could do so only with supervision. But all I wanted was nightfall, the eight o'clock distribution of pills that hastened the patients to sleep, silencing the hallways.

Xanax was valuable; I'd never considered discarding the fifty or so that remained after I recovered. I still had enough that for weeks I could avoid acknowledging the anxiety and insomnia that had characterized the onset of my previous breakdown. Soon it would be September, I told myself, the month I'd always loved best, the one that, when I was a child, had rescued me from a long season spent with my family, and offered then what I thought it would now: the solace of routine.

Our older daughter, twelve, and our son, ten, began school immediately after Labor Day. One week passed, then another. I was still waiting for a discernible lift in my spirits when, on Tuesday, September 24, our son fell ill. Although he'd never before had respiratory problems—at least not any of which we'd been aware—he was stricken with a severe asthma attack and spent five days in the hospital, three of them in pediatric ICU. Day after night after day I sat beside his bed, trying not to watch the monitor that displayed the jagged peaks and troughs of his elevated heart rate, the immediate fall in the level of oxygen in his blood when I removed his mask for a moment to untangle a snarl of tubes pulling on his IV. Treated every other hour with albuterol, a bronchodilator with stimulant side effects, my child slept little but drifted in and out of half-waking nightmares. Under the spell of one of these he screamed out in terror, and when I approached to re-assure him, he didn't recognize me, he screamed louder.

What had he seen that frightened him? I asked myself. What kind of monster?

By now I'd fallen prey to the sinister associations that can attend deepening depression. Did this explain why I failed to distinguish one oxygen mask from another? The piece of molded plastic that fit over my son's nose and mouth summoned a mask I'd seen before, another clear green one I'd adjusted just as I did his. My mother had used it to breathe when she was dying of breast cancer, choking on it, her lungs filled with metastases, her hospital bed ensnared in a similar thicket of moni-tors and coils of tubing, gleaming metal gas cocks pok-ing through the wall, a bag of blood hanging from a hook.

The chime of an IV pump, the hiss of oxygen, the unanswered telephones and endless paging of doctors, the broadcast blips of beating hearts: an electronic clamor muffled present groans and cries and returned me to my mother's bedside, to her tubes and her wires and her suffering—and to my panic at losing her before we could manage a reconciliation or even an honest farewell.

Before my son's illness, I'd congratulated myself for reaching a kind of acceptance of my tortured relationship with my mother. I'd been her only child, the baby she wasn't prepared to raise, the daughter she gave to her parents. I was the girl who loved and hated her mother in equal measure, whose longing was obvious and whose rage had always been concealed, even—especially—from herself. But I'd thought all that was behind me. I'd even told my analyst I was quitting therapy because I was increasingly bored by what had once compelled me: hashing and rehashing past agonies.

FALL 2002 was a hard season for our family, and particularly for our son. Whenever he got a little better he subsequently relapsed, relying on as many as six drugs to keep him well enough to go to school. On the worst days he was tethered to a nebulizer for hours, inhaling albuterol and a steroid called Pulmicort from the plastic mouthpiece at the end of a flexible tube. During the treatments he did homework or reread Tolkien's *Lord of the Rings*. If we let him, he watched the film version of the first book in the trilogy, *The Fellowship of the Ring*, a video we rented eleven times before buying our own copy. Over and over, our son followed a story he knew by heart, mesmerized by the struggle of good to overcome a terrifying, unknowable evil.

Having taken health for granted, our son was shocked by his new status as a sick child, sullen en route to doctor appointments, scared to go into the pool for swim class. For years he'd understood himself as an athlete, with reason. Now he worried that his Little League career and his dreams of a glorious future as a New York Yankee would be taken from him.

A detail-oriented person, I extracted some comfort from reliably managing my son's care, executing each and every doctor's order to the letter. I sat for hours before a computer screen, not working but pursuing online information about respiratory reactive disease, the clinical name for asthma. Inevitably, I strayed from the medical jargon of corporate websites into the hysteria of chat rooms, other parents' horror stories that left me reciting helpless prayers—to fate, to whatever power might keep a child from harm, to a God whose presence I couldn't feel. At bedtime I kneeled beside my son in the dark and silently invited his disease into my body.

One night, soon after he was discharged from the hospital, my son walked in his sleep, calling out for me on each stair down to the floor where my husband and I slept. Bleary with exhaustion, I assumed from the urgency of the calls that he was having another asthma attack, and that by morning we'd be back in the hospital. At breakfast my son didn't remember what had happened. But I remained sufficiently unnerved that for weeks I heard him call me in the night. Each time, I'd run upstairs to his bed and find him deeply asleep, his face erased of anxiety, his forehead dry and cool. Blue light from the street spilled over his covers, and I watched my little boy as he breathed. The stricken cries I'd heard so clearly hadn't come from my son. Though I hadn't been asleep, somehow I'd dreamed them.

Too scared to go back to my room, I would remain by his bed until morning. I'd sit in the old white rocker that had been in my own childhood bedroom, then slip away at dawn, before he could wake and find me there.

Several times a day I recorded his "peak flow," a measure of lung capacity and a critical tool for predicting, and thus preventing, asthma attacks. I graphed the readings in a booklet made for that purpose, so we could follow, hour by hour, day by day, fluctuations in our son's ability to breathe. My husband joked that the numbers on the handheld meter might just as dependably be interpreted as increments of mood—mine. The higher my son's flows, the more optimism and calm I was able to summon. When the flows dipped, even a little, I panicked. How could I explain my overreaction to my husband when I didn't understand it myself?

"I feel like this is my fault," I said, sobbing, night

after night. As soon as the children were asleep, I suc-
cumbed to the dread I'd managed, barely, to keep hidden from them. I was afraid our son would be taken
from us. From me.

"Your fault because you had asthma when you
were a child?" my husband asked, puzzled.

"Maybe," I said. But it was something else.

It had been four months before my son's hospitalization that I'd stopped nursing, relinquished that cher-
ished perception of myself as my children's primal
source of sustenance and love. Now the onset of my
son's asthma struck me as an indication of my new im-
potence. Worse, and more irrationally, it seemed to reveal me as dangerous. I saw—felt—a black, destructive
spirit, dybbuk or dervish, twisting out of my chest, a
force of corruption that sprang from me and infected
my son, choked and smothered him. Though I knew
myself to be a good mother, a loving and responsible
mother, it seemed to me that not only had I failed to
protect my child, to stand as a barrier between him and
the perils of the world, but that I'd been the inadvertent
agent of his illness. It made no sense—I did know
that—and I recognized my husband's faith in our son's
recovery as one founded on that child's underlying

health, his unusual strength. Given time, we'd learn what triggered his asthma and how to avoid or handle any future attacks. His father was sure of this. Why couldn't I be?

Again and again I returned to the nightmare my son had had in the hospital, his screams when I came to comfort him. What was it that he'd felt, or seen? A threatening presence? The opposite of what a mother should be? Of the paragon I'd tried to be in contrast to my own mother?

Seventeen when she got pregnant, my mother had allowed my father, also seventeen, to talk her out of an abortion. Perhaps a baby could help her accomplish what she hadn't on her own: escape from her jealous mother, my grandmother, who sabotaged her every attempt at independence. As she described it years later, when she was seeing a therapist, I was to have been a surrogate, a new daughter for her mother to manipulate, so that she herself could slip away. My mother married my father on his eighteenth birthday, her pregnancy too advanced to allow for a white dress or reception by those who would have been less celebrants than witnesses to her shame. Before a year had passed, she'd discarded my father and endured a nervous collapse. Attacks of agoraphobia imprisoned her in the very house she'd risked so much to escape. My mother lost the rest of her short life to protracted and never decisive battles with my grandmother, a war by turns hot and cold for which she dressed impeccably and always wore makeup, her misery—and her anger—visible in almost every family photograph.

I was thirteen when she explained how she'd used me as a stand-in for herself. Oddly, or so I thought at the time, she chose the word *hostage* to describe my role. By thirteen I was reading novels by the Brontë sisters and Dickens, even Tolstoy, so she could reasonably assume I'd understand her words, the simple transaction she described. But I reacted with dumb incomprehension, unable even to nod. Was there any age at which I could have accepted her reluctance to hold or to touch me, any rationale that might excuse the critical, sometimes disgusted eye she trained on so expensive a failure? Not only had I not purchased freedom for my mother; as it turned out, I'd spelled further entanglement. My mother, like Lot's wife, had made the mistake of looking back.

My grandparents dedicated themselves to my care. They gave me the bedroom between theirs and my mother's; they bought me clothes and paid for my private-school education. My grandmother made school lunches, wrapping sandwiches in waxed paper and placing them carefully on top of the apple so they wouldn't get squashed. Sometimes my grandfather drew a picture on the brown lunch bag, a face or an animal rendered comic by the tremor in his hand. For her part, my mother undertook to refine me, a child she'd agreed to bear and who might reflect badly on her now that I was irrevocably incarnate—a person, a life rather than an idea.

Ballet and Christian Science Sunday school, lace tights, table manners, how to walk like a lady without scuffing the shiny toes of my black Mary Janes, how to blunt my appetite with a glass of water before every meal: most of these lessons backfired. She tried and I tried, but we couldn't save me from my clumsiness, we couldn't chisel away evidence of my father, his stocky legs and studious scowl, his stubborn jaw. A thousand miles away, banished just months after my birth, he remained in sight.

I was six when my mother moved out and left me

with her parents. It was 1967, and I was in the throes of what felt like a fatal love for her. Believing in my ability to win her back, unable to reconcile myself to my abandonment, I continued to study my young mother for clues as to what—whom—she might prefer, and I worked assiduously to transform myself into that girl. But one month passed, and then another. They turned into years, and still my mother didn't come to retrieve me. She saw me on weekends, but she never packed up my toys and clothes and moved me into the little house I imagined, the one that only the two of us would share.

What did happen was that I developed asthma, my first attack following on the heels of her departure. Ever since then, I'd understood the ailment as a body's gasping in shock and grief. My son must be grieving, I'd helplessly concluded. His suffering must proceed from me, his mother—just as mine had from my mother.

"What do you mean?" my husband said. "How is that possible?"

Whatever faults my husband had discovered in me over the years, they hadn't been failures of parenting. Oh, I tended to spoil our children, but he understood this as misguided affection, the inevitable fallout of what he recognized as an unhappy childhood, and I did manage to maintain discipline along with indulgence. He wasn't inclined to praise, but my husband often said he was grateful to have married a woman who turned out to be so devoted a mother.

"He's sick because I'm bad. I'm polluted and evil and wrong. He's good, we've always said how good he is, how pure of heart, and I'm—there's something wrong with me. It's my fault he's sick."

My husband wanted to be patient, but he found what I said not only disturbing—disturbed—but infantile and narcissistic, and he told me so. I knew he was right, and acknowledged how wearying it must be for him to have yet another event in our life together shape-shift into my struggle with my mother, dead for seventeen years now, a woman my husband never met outside of my depression, which tended to recur, as might an ever-smoldering infection, when my resistance was down. To insist that this was all about me was absurdly self-involved. But knowing so didn't rescue me from the delusion. This time, even my usual defenses couldn't help me cope.

I began, each day, to eat a little less and to exercise a little more, reentering, as I always did when sufficiently threatened, the sanctuary of anorexia, that glass temple in which I hid, and which I'd first assembled in response to my mother's critical eye. To the eye that glanced off me, communicating aversion before it flicked away, betraying what looked like her wish that I didn't exist. That as long as I was there, I could at least reduce myself; make myself into a thinner, slighter, less emphatic presence.

It must seem odd to the uninitiated. How can hunger confer safety? But imagine a force of will so inexorable as to be able, gradually, painstakingly, to strip a body of flesh. Imagine the invulnerability such willpower might imply. The sudden tyranny of my son's asthma, of an illness I couldn't hope to cure, reawakened an old and dangerous fantasy, one inspired by my mother's prolonged death, a death from which I couldn't distance myself, a death that, given our dire identification, felt like my own. While my mother suffered horribly, I had assuaged my bedside panic with anorexia, disease masquerading as remedy. If I could prevail over what sickened and died—the body, the greedy and demanding body—then couldn't I also prevail over the death that awaited me, that awaited everyone? Even, and most unbearably, the three children I loved.

And if I couldn't pull off so powerful and absolute a spell, maybe I could manage a less ambitious one, that of substitutive suffering: mine in trade for theirs?

Once I'd forced these magical thoughts into consciousness, I expected to vanquish them and imagined how swiftly they would break down and evaporate, like movie vampires dragged from the dark into the light. But over and over I failed to recognize the power of irrational hopes, wishes held so tightly and for so long that I'd grown up around them. I admitted their impossibility, but I couldn't excise them any more easily than I could pull out nails long driven into a tree, each season a little more of them swallowed by the trunk's increasing diameter.

One Sunday morning, when I was fifteen, I hid my face in my hands to spit out the Communion wafer the priest had placed on my tongue, abandoning one religion for another. Anorexia had become the belief system in which I invested my fiercest longings, nonsense that couldn't be banished by sense any more than could the central and implausible tenet of Catholicism—Resurrection. Starving was a form of prayer. Focused, consecrated, private, for twenty-six years it had seen me through periods of strain. All it took to relapse was my heightened awareness that I couldn't influence fate, that all I loved was fragile and impermanent: every thing, every life, and even love itself.

I lost a few pounds, and then a few more. I regressed even so far as my adolescent habit of taking any private opportunity to unbutton my clothes before a mirror, to reassure myself with my reflection, bones I took care not to let my husband see. But this time anorexia didn't deliver; at least it hadn't so far. I wasn't feeling safe or in control.

Nor did my scrupulous response to our son's newly diagnosed allergies lessen my fear. I ordered seven hundred dollars' worth of products from an allergy-management catalog, dusted his room compulsively, mite-proofed his bedding, and treated his carpet with a stinging borate solution that claimed to inhibit dust-mite infestation. A regimen was established. The two doors to his room were kept shut, and the new HEPA air filter ran continuously. His older sister walked through his room, sniffing long, deep, exaggerated sniffs.

"What are you doing?" I asked her.

"I'm experiencing really clean air."

By now my daughter was tired of having her needs come third, after her ailing brother's and her baby sister's. Still, her reproaches were essentially good-humored and generous. She was kind to me, my watchful eldest child. From birth it had seemed her intent to provide the antidote to long-ago hurts. "You smell so good," she'd tell me, pressing her nose into my neck, "like toast," words that annulled those of my mother, who advised me never to waste my money on expensive fragrances. Shalimar was my favorite, but when I wore it around her she'd wrinkle her nose. There was something about my body chemistry, she said, that turned perfume "rancid."

My daughter pointed her nose toward the ceiling and inhaled deeply. She released her breath with an *ahhhhh*, and I smiled to accept her ribbing. Usually, I'm the first to laugh at my excesses and quirks, and give myself ample occasion to do so. But I was too panicked and pessimistic to find anything funny in this campaign.

On more than one occasion I wept in front of a doctor, and I spent many private hours pacing and wringing my hands. Each day while my son trudged the short distance home from school, I watched for him at an upstairs window, trying to ascertain the state of his health from the rate of his steps, the tilt of his head. For all of October and November I arranged my schedule to make sure that I was home every day at 3:10, often only to leave soon thereafter, saving errands to occupy my afternoons, because being near my son made me cry. I worried that even if I stayed behind the door of my study, my presence in our house would have a negative impact on his health. My anxiety was so palpable, it would taint the air he breathed, disrupt the flow of energy, further tax his strength. The only friend with whom I shared my hysteria urged me, with increasing insistence, to contact my analyst and to consider going back on antidepressants.

If only I were nursing. It wouldn't help my son, but it might stop me from going crazy. Then I began to wonder: why?

On a Sunday when my husband was out of town and my older daughter was at a friend's house, the sliding door to my son's bedroom got stuck. I couldn't close it. This had happened before; all that was required to fix the door was gently rocking it back onto its track. But I couldn't do it this time. I lacked forbearance, balance. When I'm nervous I'm clumsy. I lose touch with my body and mismanage spatial relationships.

There was a hammer on the shelf, and I used it to tap the door, top and bottom, but I couldn't budge it. Immediately I flew into a raging tantrum, hurled myself at the door, pulled on the old glass knob, pounded and cursed. It was only when I struck the knob so hard that it broke, gashing my middle finger, that I stopped, gratified by the sight of my blood, gratified and calmed. *Good,* I thought, watching it run down my wrist. *Bleed,* I thought.

My son and younger daughter stared at me from the adjoining room, silent and amazed. I had never before behaved like this in front of them, or anyone. "Sorry," I said. "I'm really sorry. Mom's stressed-out. Stressed-out, that's all."

"About what?" my son asked carefully. He knew— he must have known, for he knows me through and through—that the answer was at least in part him, the asthma.

"Work," I lied. "I'm behind. I missed a deadline."

Downstairs, I sat on the bathroom floor and watched the cut saturate a wad of tissues. I pulled back the flap of skin to assess its depth. Already I understood my paroxysm: the door was stuck so I couldn't close it; I couldn't seal off my son's room and run the HEPA filter; I couldn't make sure the air was clean, couldn't protect him from invisible threat. I'd lost it—control, the fraying ability to keep myself in line.

The next day I took the X-Acto knife out of my desk drawer and put it downstairs, far from my reach. Anorexia was one thing; being comforted by the appearance of my blood was another.

I called my analyst, the one I'd seen for ten years, the one I stopped seeing the last time I was pregnant, when, buoyed by the life I carried, I grew impatient with examining old wounds and graduated myself prematurely. "I need to talk to you," I told her.

Because my analyst had recently had a knee replacement, she was working out of her apartment, a place I'd never visited. My years of weekly treatment had been conservative, formal, and necessarily one-sided. My analyst was as strict as she was sympathetic, and in all that time we had never embraced, had rarely touched. I was afraid to see her home because I preferred her unknown and unknowable. My relationship with my own mother had been damaging enough that, forty-one years old, I remained vulnerable to older women, prone to fervent attachment and unreasonable hurt. In my analyst's carefully polished therapeutic mirror I'd found the reflection of wishes and fears long hidden. I'd depended on its clarity and did not want it tarnished; nor did I want to be given any snag on which my neediness might catch.

As it turned out, I hardly saw the apartment. The sight of her face—the proximity of help—was so potent a catalyst for tears that I saw nothing.

"You know you need to be on medication," she said, after I'd told her about the past two months, admitting everything: the obsessive worrying; the unwarranted conviction that I had made my son sick; the insomnia; the fear of annihilation that plagued me; the seductive calm offered by the sight of my blood; the complex of rules pertaining to food, a quagmire from which I'd nearly escaped again and again, more times than I could count.

"You're not forgetting what happened before," my analyst prompted, alluding to my stubborn refusal, in 1998, to resort to antidepressants, pride that insisted I deny depression until it dismantled me.

"No," I said. "I remember."

We scheduled an appointment for the following week, and in the meantime I saw my internist to get prescriptions for Paxil (an SSRI that relieves anxiety), Wellbutrin (a mood elevator), and enough Xanax to tide me over during the weeks before the first two took effect. It was a familiar arsenal. Together my doctor and I acknowledged that I was thin; there was ten pounds less of me than there had been six months before, when I'd had my yearly physical. But, expecting the drugs to do their job, we didn't belabor the observation.

In the month before the antidepressants kicked in,

I had a few panic attacks, a blight I recognized from my earlier breakdown. At least I no longer mistook them for cardiac arrest or cerebral hemorrhages or organ failure. These did have the new feature of beginning with a burning sensation all over my body, as if every inch of my skin had been scoured with BenGay. Then my heart beat fast, faster, too fast—it would have to stop or break. Floors tilted, ceilings pressed down, menacing swaths of red swung open and shut like phantom theater curtains, showing me either too much or too little. Language and music refused to cohere into anything I could understand but came at me broken into scrambled, mocking bits. And the attacks lasted an hour or more, long enough to drench my clothes and hair with sweat, fold me into a fetal position, and leave me witless.

Each time I saw my analyst, we reviewed my son's improving health and then, inevitably, returned to the subject of breast-feeding, and the depression that had arrived in May, when I'd stopped nursing and lost a bond that, I'd begun to admit, protected and soothed me as much as it had my children. Without nursing—without the hope of ever nursing again—I had a sense of being stalked by a black, destructive force. My son's illness suggested to me that this invisible predator was drawing closer. It was only a matter of time before it got me. But what was the black force? As had previous fears, this one dragged our conversations back to what I called my "failure to connect" with my mother.

"Your mother was a sadist," my analyst said at the end of one session as she closed her notebook and capped her pen.

Too shocked to respond in the moment, I silently rehearsed retorts throughout the following week, planning an opening salvo for our next appointment. I had explanations, justifications—a hundred excuses my mother never offered. She was too young to have had a child, so young that she'd even lied to me about her age, claiming to have been nineteen when I was born. I never did the math until after she died, and when I did I was sure I must have been mistaken. Over and over I subtracted her birth date from mine, March 1961 minus September 1942. In fact, she'd been eighteen. What a sad little cheat she had devised, tacking on six months, a few paper pages of a calendar. I felt a visceral twist of pity when I thought of my mother trying to hide her youth behind so flimsy a disguise.

And if she'd always been late to pick me up from school or church or ballet, it was because she'd been disorganized, not cruel. She couldn't have known what it was like to wait for hours with the Russian dance teacher and her swift, stinging yardstick. I'd sit on the floor in the corner of the mirrored studio—a girl so clumsy that often when I danced the teacher didn't have to slap me with her stick, I fell over it. Still wearing a leotard and tights, I'd wrap my arms around my knees and watch as Madame taught one after another class. *She'll be here, she'll be here, another five minutes and she'll be here.* But I didn't believe my mantra. Afraid I'd be left forever with this martinet who hated me, her most unpromising student, I'd eventually succumb to tears and hide my face in my knees.

But how could my mother have guessed this when she'd been good at ballet, so good that before she'd gotten pregnant she'd considered dance as a career? She'd been the kind of girl who would have rejoiced at extra hours in a dance studio, and I'd always been too ashamed to tell her that I'd cried, ashamed and frightened. My mother got angry when I cried in public. My tears seemed to accuse her, she said. People might assume she was unkind or untrustworthy.

But surely an occasional slap across the face didn't amount to sadism.

"In this room we don't judge," I told my analyst. "That's what you've always said. You've always said it was counterproductive. Calling my mother a sadist was unfair. It was insulting. You didn't know her. If she was your patient, if she told everything the way she saw it, then you'd be on her side.

"Just because I was a child doesn't mean I was the only one who suffered. We've talked about how I hurt her. How I tried to be my grandmother's good girl and took advantage of their always fighting. Ingratiated myself with my stupid A's and A pluses.

"And before that, before I came along, she had her own problems.

"Anyway, doesn't sadism imply conscious cruelty? A conscious intent to inflict cruelty? Whatever she did, my mother didn't . . . she didn't set out to damage me. Whatever happened, happened in the moment—it wasn't premeditated."

My analyst listened as I ranted, and then she apologized. She smiled, and I couldn't tell if she was trying to soften the harsh impression she'd made or if she was amused.

CHRISTMAS was five days away, and I no longer dreaded it. I'd been on antidepressants for a month when, abruptly, pleasure returned. All that had been dull shined; even the commonplace beckoned. Pigeons pecked crumbs, and I couldn't dismiss the sheen of their quick heads—no more exalted than a prism of oil on a puddle, and no less luminous.

On the way home from my analyst's, I stopped to look at an Oriental rug hanging in a store window on Broadway. Dark blue, light blue, scarlet, orange: who could have woven such complex and beautiful geometry? It was as if God flew out of the pattern and into my face, pressing tears from my eyes. I stood so close to the glass that my breath fogged it. My little boy would be okay, and somehow, so would I.

"Do other people feel like this all the time?" I asked my husband, filled with wonder. We were standing at the kitchen counter, and he turned to look at me.

"Yes," he said. "I think they do."

For months I'd managed, despite my anxiety, to function. I'd done laundry and I'd cooked dinner. I'd presided over homework and baths. I'd read bedtime stories. I'd deflected my older daughter's scrutiny with quips and caresses, hugged the younger one for the reassurance I could give her, and then hugged her again for the feel of her warm body in my arms.

Somehow I'd gotten my son to all of his doctors' appointments, bribing him into polished lobbies and up medical-plaza elevators, leading him on with baseball cards, first five packs, then ten, twenty. The two of us sat beside each other in the waiting-room chairs, and sometimes he let me hold his hand. I watched him open each pack of cards, hoping for a good one, the sliver of comfort it might buy.

But being a mother, a good enough mother, was all I'd managed to be. I hadn't written even half of what I'd hoped to complete. And I hadn't been the wife I'd wanted to be for my husband, hadn't been able to offer him the calm and self-contained presence I'd planned for this period when he was working full-time while finishing the final draft of a novel. Even so casual a question as "How's it going?" invited tears I couldn't stop.

"I guess I should have come with a disclaimer," I said. "Something that might have warned you off. But I didn't really know. Before we were married I didn't really know that I'd . . . well, that I'd . . ."

"Oh," he said. "You did. You did warn me."

"Did I? When?"

"You told me you'd been treated for depression. Don't you remember? We talked about it."

I looked into my husband's face. "Yes, but we didn't—you didn't—really know what that meant. We didn't know it would come back."

"No," he said, "we didn't." He shrugged and pulled me toward him, into his arms. "But then we didn't know about me, either." Gallantly, my husband began to list his own failings and invited me to join him.

"*It?*" my analyst asked over and over. "What? What is *it?*"

"I don't know. I don't know. It's black. And vindictive. It wants to destroy me. *Me* in particular."

I wasn't depressed, but neither was I well. Anxious, restless, compulsive, I couldn't sleep without Xanax, and I woke with a start as soon as it wore off.

"Are you eating?" my analyst asked.

"I'm doing my best, sort of scraping along, a few hundred calories under the mark. You know how stubborn anorexia is, how intractable. Nothing makes me feel as armored." Ironic, as my husband had pointed out innumerable times—ironic and perverse to find safety in a behavior, an addiction, that undermined my health.

But my analyst just nodded. After all, she'd known me for years now, during which I'd characterized my eating disorder as a shatterproof glass box. I was inside, alone and safe. I could see out, and nothing could get in. I admitted that the invisible boundary separated me from the touch of other people; I admitted that the box had no door; I admitted that anorexia was a maladaptation; and I admitted, with chagrin, to more than two decades of remissions mistaken for recoveries. There were good years, and there were bad; in either case, it was a rare day that I went to bed unaware of the number of calories I'd consumed. Except when I was pregnant; then I understood my body as belonging to someone else, and I cared for it as I would a borrowed book.

Through January and half of February my analyst and I deconstructed the disease once again. If it offered safety, then safety from what? What was the black and predatory *it*?

At home, my husband alternately cajoled and complained. During breakfast he slipped a chocolate cookie onto my spartan plate. When we sat down for dinner, he scowled across the table at my forkful of salad. Some nights, after the children were asleep, he harangued me. I looked older when I was so thin. I looked less attractive. He preferred depression to anorexia, which he found repellent and infuriating.

"I'm working on it," I said. "Would that it were as simple as vanity."

I wasn't really trying, he accused. In any case, whatever I said about making an effort was worthless. Anorexia inspired dishonesty. What wouldn't I say to protect my addiction? As far as he was concerned, not eating enough was no different from and no better than drinking too much or abusing drugs, and he wanted me to quit, now, tonight. Yesterday.

At my analyst's urging, I returned to my internist. I expected nothing more serious than a quick scold. After all, in November I'd escaped without a lecture. I could go home and tell my husband everything was fine. I was skinny, but so what? I'd been skinny before.

My internist, however, someone I regarded as a gifted physician as well as an uncommonly gracious person, looked at me and frowned.

"I know I'm thin," I said.

"Thinner. Take your shoes off." He directed me onto the scale.

"So," he said when I stepped off, "what's this?" Arms crossed, eyes on mine, he wasn't his affable self.

I shrugged. "Uh, the, you know . . . it's an old problem." Compared with the more overtly self-destructive behavior that resulted, four years earlier, in my hospitalization, anorexia seemed of a lesser magnitude. As my referring physician, he'd known details of that breakdown—the voice no one else heard calling for my death, my attempts to placate it with lesser sacrifices. Why was he being so dour now, when I was medicated and coherent? "It's been way worse than this," I said. "At least fifteen pounds worse. Maybe twenty."

"Congratulations," he said, sarcastic. "That's just great. Something to be proud of." He reviewed the statistics: 10 to 15 percent mortality. He listed dangers to my heart, to my immune system, to my bones, already thinned as a result of Graves' disease. Leaning toward me, he used his index finger to trace the sharp line of my cheekbone from the outer corner of my eye back toward my ear.

"Oh, come on," I said, pulling away, "even if I weighed one-fifty, I'd have an angular face."

He shook his head. "Not like this. There's a clinical term for this. It's called temporal wasting." *Temporal*, I thought, defining it incorrectly as *temporary*, a problem that would resolve itself and, with time, cease to trouble me. But in fact it referred to the temporal bone, visible because the flesh that should cloak it had wasted away.

My doctor folded his arms over my chart and contemplated me with an expression I'd seen on my husband's face when he was in our garden, deliberating just where to drive a stake into the earth, where to prop or tie a branch. A look reserved for trees that had grown awry, it conveyed more distress than reproach. Ashamed, I dropped my eyes.

"I don't want to be paternalistic," he said, and his voice wasn't stern but weary. "I don't like being put in this position. But someone has to draw a line in the sand."

"How do you mean?" I asked, hearing the guarded tone of my voice. He named a weight three pounds below my current reading on his scale. "What happens if I go under?"

"I put you in the hospital. They put a tube down your nose and force-feed you." He recited a recent horror story of another career anorexic. Two desperate, aged parents had brought in their thirty-nine-year-old daughter, whom they ended up declaring incompetent to save her life. My internist would see me in a month, he said, when I could look forward to stepping back on his scale. And by the way, in case I'd forgotten, he hadn't: I was due for my annual bone scan at the beginning of May.

I left his office in a state of agitation that even all the medication I was on didn't diminish. One month, four weeks, a three-pound margin. A hospital stay with a tube in my nose—no one had threatened such a punishment for decades. I'd run out of time to solve this problem. *My daughter, my daughter, just thirteen.* The words made an endless loop in my head; I couldn't turn them off.

During the years after I'd weaned my son and before I was pregnant with our second daughter I'd managed to keep my eating disorder mostly in check. Afraid of setting an injurious example for my older daughter, I'd willed it into less objectionable compulsions, with less observable effects. I'd been a vegan. I'd been a health crank. I'd fixated on carrot juice and non-genetically modified soy. I'd run ten miles a day, depending on garlic supplements to protect my joints as I spent enough cartilage to purchase knee surgery. There'd been a bad patch in 1998, the year I was hospitalized for depression, but my older daughter was only eight at the time—still young enough, I'd prayed, to see me through the undiscriminating lens of early childhood. She and her brother, then six, had seemed to accept whatever reasons my husband had given for my absence, and for my being somewhere children weren't allowed to visit. This time, when I could no longer disguise how thin I was, I anticipated my older daughter's concern and told her my thyroid balance was off, a credible lie since 1996, when I had been diagnosed with Graves' disease. But what could disguise a tube in my nose? And my husband—oh God, my husband would be livid. Frightened and thus very, very angry.

PLEASE," I begged my analyst. "I'm scared. I'm scared. I have to find a way out of this. You have to help me." She looked at me, and I at her. I'd decided on our first session in November that I wouldn't lie on her couch this time around. I needed to see her face.

"It's like I'm in this black hole and the sides are too high for me to climb out," I heard myself say. How quickly my glass box had changed. What had been clear and filled with light—imagine Snow White in her shining casket, too beautiful to bury, waiting for resurrection—had suddenly been revealed as a different sort of tomb, dark and claustrophobic, a death that offered no possibility of rebirth. "I want your hand, I want your hand," I begged. "Please help me. I need you." I watched her eyes.

"I'm here," my analyst said. "I'm right here."

"I'm ready to admit something," I told her, and I started to cry.

"Yes?" she said. "What?"

"*It*. It's my mother." She nodded, and so did I. "I know we both knew that all along," I said. "I know you did, anyway, and that I knew it somewhere, but it was a place in my head I couldn't get to before. Because . . . because I was scared. And now, well, I'm still scared. But I can't afford her anymore. It's been years, so many years since she died, and all that time I've embraced her. Remade her. Inside myself. Refused to let her go. And it's not even *her*—I can't even say I know who my mother, who the real woman, was. The thing in me is . . . is a . . . an impression left over from when I don't even remember." The black dybbuk who tore out of my breast, who threatened to kill my son.

My second confession was that, despite my insistence on its many saving graces, breast-feeding, whose loss I mourned to the point of depression, was not the purely benign, innocent, and saintly occupation I'd made out.

"Alleluia," my analyst said, a word I'd never heard her use before. I stared as she looked heavenward and lifted her hands in a gesture of charismatic praise.

No, nursing was tricky, it was duplicitous. A gift to my children, it had also been a means of rebuking my mother, the dark and murdering mother I'd hidden within myself, the mother who had put me on a diet when I was seven and taken my milk away. "You can still have skim," she said, but I refused any substitute. I wanted the whole, the fat. I wanted milk that left a thick coat of itself on the lip of my glass. Half a life later, when I was nursing and expressing my own milk to freeze, each time I filled a bottle I'd tilt it to see the fat as it rose and formed a generous layer on top—to see what I'd taken from my body for the good of my babies. I'd used nursing to pare myself down, exulted in an effortless alchemy that transformed my essence into milk. "I can't help losing weight," I'd lie during the months of breast-feeding, never admitting that often I didn't eat the extra calories it required, that I intended for my body to accuse my mother, testify to my having given the pound of flesh she'd withheld.

Dead, a citizen of the underworld, endowed with its privileges and powers, my mother had become not less but more of a presence. Dead, she wielded influence and commanded whole aspects of me. She wasn't a woman any longer but an immortal, a mercurial goddess who regretted having given me life. But long before I could acknowledge how fiercely she possessed me, I'd instinctively placed my nursing body as a barrier between her and my babies, in whom I'd tried to resurrect the little girl I had been, cradle and feed my young self as I had not been cradled or fed.

"So how will we use your new knowledge?" my analyst asked, pen and notebook at the ready. "How will it help us?"

"So far at least I haven't fucked them up," I said, referring to my children, as I have throughout the years of analysis. My arrival at motherhood has necessarily been a big topic. "Against the odds, I've managed to be a good mother."

"So far," she agreed. And then she did something unprecedented, astonishing: she yelled at me. In defiance of her proper self, the generally stringent manners of this woman in her seventies, she said another word I'd never heard her use before. She said the word *fuck*. "You haven't fucked them up, but you're fucking yourself up! You're destroying yourself, and that will fuck up your children! It will fuck up everyone you love!"

As soon as she raised her voice, I put my hands over my face, afraid to see the source of such anger, returned without warning to the child I was at five or seven, nine, ten, eleven, twelve . . . paralyzed by my mother's rage, unable to answer or move. Eyes closed, head ducked, I felt what I hadn't for years—the velvety, blinding, black safety of that hole into which I used to tumble, subterranean like a well, or a grave. There was a time when I could stay there for hours, feeling nothing, not even the beat of my heart.

"What?" my analyst said when, after a few minutes, I hadn't moved or spoken. "Where have you gone? What are you thinking?"

Answering required keeping my eyes closed, my hands over my face. "Please," I whispered, "it scares me when you yell."

"I've stopped," she said gently. And then, after more time had passed and I remained silent, unmoving, "I'm not your mother. I'm never going to abandon you. I don't do that. For as long as you want me, I'm here to help you."

I forced my hands into my lap but left my eyes closed. "If she wants me dead," I said, "if that's what would satisfy her, if that's the form she'd like me to assume, then I'll do it for her. It's always been a way of doing it for her—of having at least that much control."

I'd leave behind an empty body. I'd always been able to see it so clearly, could picture my stomach, empty as a purse that had never been used, the hollow, pink coils of my intestines, innocent of food, cleaner than a newborn's. The body that I'd denied food, because she wanted it erased, a mistake she'd made. I could be undone, couldn't I? And all the rest with me: her shotgun marriage, aborted education, ruined romantic career? Her failure to escape from her own mother's grip?

"That way I get to have vengeance," I said. "In the end it wouldn't be that she'd taken back the life she gave me, but that I had taken it away from her. Exposed her as the enemy she was. Even if the act was accomplished with my help, everyone would know who she really was. Who she was to me." I opened my eyes. "I have to get away from her. I have to get her out of me. But how? How can I stand to lose my mother?"

My analyst shook her head. For a minute or more she looked at me without speaking. Then, "Can you tell me why separating from her feels so impossible?" she asked. "Can you tell me what frightens you about the idea? After all, you've identified her as your enemy."

"Who would I be without my mother? All my life I've understood myself as her child, as the child who strove to make her love me. Without her, there'd be all this . . . this room left over inside. I'd be . . . I'd be lonely."

"*Lonely?*" Usually careful to maintain her analyst's poker face, she looked mystified. The box of tissues was empty, and I dried my eyes with my shirt.

"Inside myself," I tried to explain. "Alone inside myself."

"If you're alone," she said, "and I don't believe you are, but *if*, it's because you allow your mother to stand between you and all the genuine love in your life. Think of your family, your husband and your children. Think of your friends. Then there's you—you in your glass box, your black hole—whatever you want to call it." Did she sound fed up, or was I projecting my own disgust? "I think," she said, after a silence, "I think we should stop for today. I think it might be better if we didn't go any further."

Assuming she meant I should get up and collect my coat and gloves, leave twenty minutes early, I felt chastened, dismissed, and I was trying to muster the courage to say so when she continued. "We'll have a Quaker meeting. We'll sit together in silence, and if either of us is inspired to speak, then she will."

Familiar with the faith's practice, I nodded. My husband is a Quaker, and we were married in a Quaker meeting. For many years my analyst has served as a

Quaker school's consulting psychologist. She looked at me, and I managed to return her gaze for a minute, then closed my eyes.

Who was my mother? Not the mother-memory within me, but the real person, the dybbuk's namesake. Much of what I'd inferred about the woman, who had always avoided intimacies—at least with me—came through having become a mother myself. I knew how relentless a baby's needs might seem to an eighteen-year-old, and how a first-grader could well discourage dates. But having children had also deepened my confusion about the past, and sharpened my resentment. Because I enjoyed the company of my children as I did no one else's, wanted them as I did no one else, because my children had brought me joy I'd never imagined, I wondered not so much why but *how* my mother could have left me.

And how was I to let her go? How, when letting go was admitting defeat, accepting what I'd refused all my life, that I'd failed. I was never going to be what or who she wanted.

Under my closed lids, I saw water, bodies in water. Ophelia, as painted by the Pre-Raphaelite Sir John Everett Millais, lying on her back in a stream, her palms upturned as if in prayer, departed if not yet dead. Flowers float among the folds of her splendid dress; tendrils of her hair mingle with strands of eelgrass. The artist caught her just before she was carried away by her mad anguish.

A photograph I'd seen in a gallery, black and white, the ghostly outline of a body beneath the surface of a lake, water that mirrored the clouds even as it revealed a corpse.

Varanasi, a city my husband and I visited on our honeymoon in India, and where we saw a body as it was fed to the fire on Manikarnika, the burning ghat on the bank of the Ganges. Wrapped in white linen and heaped with marigolds, it caught quickly; the bright flames leapt up. Men wearing only loincloths squatted in a circle around the hissing, blackened bundle, their heads newly shorn. Husband, sons, and brothers of the dead, they talked quietly to one another as flesh shrank into ash. At one point, the corpse's arm ligaments contracted and tightened from the heat; a slender black hand rose from the pyre, waved slowly, and fell. A Dom poked the embers with his pole. Behind him, the sacred river shrugged under her mantle of sparks.

At dawn the next morning, under an orange sky,

my husband and I rowed on the rippling, orange Ganges. A pale and nearly naked corpse floated silently past our boat, trailing her winding sheet, close enough to touch. She slipped under the purple shadow cast by one of our dripping, stilled oars; it flickered over her chest, her throat, her eyes, and then she was off, growing smaller, nearly gone.

Image after image of departure, of a woman's body carried away from me as I remained on shore: tranquil scenes, and beautiful. I described them to my analyst, listening with interest to what I was saying. All through this session I'd heard myself speak what I hadn't yet thought. This happens in therapy, of course—unconscious erupts into conscious—but never had my discoveries been so revealing, or so directive.

"I know what I have to do," I told my analyst. "It's something I considered years ago, but I must not have been ready."

"What is it?"

"I'm going to have my mother disinterred. She's buried in Los Angeles, and I'm going to have her dug up, cremated, and sent here. Then I'm going to scatter the ashes into the water. Into a river, or into the sea. I'm going to say good-bye."

My analyst nodded. "I think that might be a very good idea," she said.

My husband agreed. "It sounds right, somehow. I'm not sure why exactly." But he knows as well as I do how important ritual is. We've joked about my tendency toward magical thinking—my study filled with icons and relics, with candle stubs bearing witness to fervid prayer—but we're both writers, after all, and symbols are our stock-in-trade. It's our job to invest the material with the ineffable.

"I don't want you to talk about this with the children," my husband said. "And I don't want to know any more about it either. I don't want to know when she . . . when it arrives."

"What do you think I'm planning to do? Install her on the mantel? I'd never say anything about this to the children. It's between the two of us only. Between my mother and me."

"Maybe," he qualified, "I should know the, um, parameters, the approximate date."

I looked at him. "In case I start acting weird?" He raised his eyebrows. "Weirder, I mean?"

My husband sighed. "I just think this may be harder than you know."

"All right," I said.

But I was excited, almost elated. Already, I'd begun to anticipate the arrival of my mother's ashes as I would a gift, not a tribulation. They were what I needed to cast her away from myself. Nothing else could support the weight of meaning I intended for them to bear. Determined to have our parting accomplished by March 20, when I would turn forty-two, I began looking through files for the documents I would need.

Forty-two is a charged number for me. At forty-two my grandmother was pregnant for the first time— with my mother. Both of my parents were born in 1942. It was when she was forty-two that my mother's breast cancer metastasized and that she began, unambiguously, to die. Perhaps, at that same age, I could begin to live as I hadn't before.

I CALLED the parish church my mother used to attend, the one where her funeral was held. I hadn't been able to remember its name for years, and it wasn't in any of my files, but it came to me when I was on the subway, returning home from my analyst's—Saint Cyril's. The church secretary told me that the San Fernando Mission cemetery was the one most likely to have interred my mother's body.

Mission, I thought. *Mission Hills.* Yes, that was where we'd gone to bury her, that was where her body was.

The woman who answered the cemetery office's phone put me on hold; a few minutes later, another woman's voice came on the line. It would take her a while to look up records from 1985, she said. They were old enough to have been moved to a separate building. Would it be all right if she called me back in an hour or so?

I went upstairs. As if under a spell, I opened the top drawer of my bureau and took out lingerie, old slips and camisoles of my mother's, most of which I'd never worn but had kept among my own since her death. I put them in a shopping bag to drop off at the local Salvation Army, hunted through my closet for whatever else I'd inherited from her: a pullover; an evening jacket; two cardigan sweaters; a black velvet dress I'd stepped into and buttoned and, when I saw myself in the mirror, taken off, at least once each winter since her death. I folded these and put them in the bag. Then I dumped my clutch of cosmetics out on the bathroom counter and extracted a compact of rouge, a concealer stick, and three eye pencils—also my mother's—and threw them away.

Like the lingerie, like the clothes I'd packed and unpacked through four changes of address, I'd kept her makeup with my own, seeing and touching and sometimes using it. Now I understood why I'd never told anyone of these daily communions: they were perverse, and on some level I'd known that anyone would judge them so.

During the following week, as I spoke daily with cemetery and mortuary personnel, requesting forms I needed, finding out the cost to disinter, cremate, and ship remains from Los Angeles to New York, my peaceful vision of a body floating away on a leisurely, lullaby tide changed. It became violent; it answered my perennial fascination with spilling blood; it reflected the deeper, older savagery I felt toward my mother. Fury I'd denied, because what evidence I'd found of it over the years—always in retrospect, always the scorched earth, never the flames—terrified me.

"I'm not so much having my mother dug out of the ground as I am exhuming her from my own body," I told my analyst.

I described the operation I'd imagined. "I see myself on a metal table, under bright lights. The two halves of my rib cage are pulled apart by one of those spreading devices used for open-heart surgery. No one else is with me. There isn't any surgeon. I reach into myself and tear her out, a black lump, with these roots, twisted and sinister. Like a tumor, sort of."

Seventeen years before, I hadn't simply had my mother buried under a green blanket of sod. I'd entombed her in my own breast, where she lived and fed off me, where I kept her alive so that I could keep trying, so that one day I could demonstrate my worth. She'd have to concede—I would force her to concede—that at last I had answered her desire, at last I'd made myself into a daughter she could love. The past wouldn't have been redeemed so much as refuted. X-ed out. Rewritten with me in the role of the victor.

My earliest memory of my mother was of her hands pushing me out of her lap. We were in the garden, on a lawn chair, and it was sunny. "Get off," she said. "You're too heavy. You're going to make varicose veins." *Varicose.* What a menacing, black, and unknowable word. It slid before the sun, and the day turned dark. My shock and hurt at that moment were feelings I'd examined many times. But now I remembered more. I recalled not what I'd forgotten but the part of the story I'd always failed to retrieve, the part that proved my inability, even as a small child, to forgive my mother. I left the garden and hid in the cool garage. In the shadows, I breathed the familiar, comforting smells of gasoline and rubber. Leaning against the fender of my grandmother's long blue sedan, I thought the ugliest thoughts I could—that my mother wasn't nice, she wasn't pretty, that her lap prickled where she shaved her thighs for dates, that she deserved whatever punishment *varicose* meant. That if I couldn't stop myself from loving her, I'd learn to hate her just as hard.

When my analyst asked me why I'd always ab-horred the idea of my mother's body lying embalmed in a box underground, I said I found it "impossible." I couldn't tolerate her being down there indefinitely.

"Indefinitely?" she asked, loading the question with the tone of her voice.

"Yes. Forever."

I heard my words and understood. I didn't feel what I'd always told myself I felt—pity for her lonely, cancer-struck body. No, I couldn't stand the idea of the mother I'd failed to please resting in her casket, biding her time. Never dust unto dust but sleeping forever on a white satin pillow. Waiting for the kiss of some sty-gian prince to wake her, to bring her and the agony of her censure back.

How clear everything had become, how suddenly, weirdly obvious. And throughout the last months of therapy I'd been complaining that I couldn't see enough to help myself out of the mess I was in.

No, no. Not at all. Happens all the time," the mortuary director at San Fernando Mission said when I wondered aloud if my request was unusual. "People relocate. They want their loved ones nearby." His voice managed to be both unctuous and abrasive, filing off every conversational bump. "You're bringing your mother home to be with you," he said.

"Yes, exactly," I lied smoothly.

I faxed him those documents required to exhume my mother's casket: her death certificate, and my grandmother's (to prove that I was the only living kin), the contract for the purchase of the plot in which my mother was buried, and a formal letter detailing my request. In return came forms to sign and bills to pay, a total of $3,846.34 for the permit to disinter, disinterment, casket disposal, cremation, shipping container, transit permit, and shipping. The release of plot G121 to the cemetery allowed a credit of $386.75, adjusting the debt to $3,459.59. My mother's second funeral would cost $1,241.94 more than her first.

But if I could ransom myself for a few thousand dollars, wouldn't that be an economy, especially when compared with a failure as expensive as my mother's attempt to free herself from my grandmother? *Ransom* had been her word, the word that went with *hostage*. "You were supposed to ransom me," she'd said when she'd figured it out—the reason she'd consented not to have an abortion.

When the paperwork was completed, my notarized signatures received, the mortuary director called. "Okay," he said. "We're all set here."

"You said you accept MasterCard?"

"And Visa. American Express."

"Talk to me!" my younger daughter screamed in the background. "Me! Me! Me!"

"I can picture her," he said. "A cherub. A darling."

The cherub cackled and ripped off her wet training pants. She threw them. I ducked. Experimentally, she bit the back of my thigh. This daughter was a child who believed the insult of her mother's absorption in a phone call warranted extreme measures, a child who believed in action. I kissed her and climbed from a chair up onto the low dresser, mostly out of her reach, leaving her my toes to tug. "Just a minute, only a minute more," I promised her.

"About the necklace?" I asked the mortician, after the credit verification came through.

"I haven't forgotten. It's here in the file." He exhaled loudly, as if exasperated. I could hear his breath against the receiver. "I always tell people, don't bury the jewelry. Keep it. There's a treasure chest out there."

"Very pragmatic," I said, trying to sound sincere, picturing countless gems hidden where they couldn't twinkle, under a skin of sod. "But this necklace has little material value. It's just a cross and a religious medal."

What I didn't tell him was that I didn't want it for sentiment so much as for proof, assurance that it was my mother whose casket had been opened, whose body had been burned.

"I'm going to do her myself," the mortician said. "And I promise you, if it's at all possible, I'll retrieve your necklace. We disinfect, of course."

Now that it was happening, I was frightened. The Xanax I took to fall asleep wore off by four A.M., and at that hour I found myself sitting up in bed, my heart racing as if I'd been caught committing a crime. I almost expected that the streetlight coming through the shutters would reveal blood on my hands. Four was too late to take another pill; if I did, I might not wake in time to get my children off to school. So I got up and showered. I made coffee, tried to read. By the time the rest of the family joined me at the breakfast table, I was calm, or at least calm enough not to call attention to myself.

But on February 26, after I was notified that my mother's disinterment and cremation were scheduled for the following Monday, March 3, guilt began to torment me all day. In the midst of an innocent occupation, even one I enjoyed, like walking my younger daughter to nursery school, my heart would quicken. Sirens startled me as they never had before. When I passed a police officer on the sidewalk I couldn't meet his eye.

It didn't help to remind myself that my mother had died of cancer, that this had happened years before, and that arranging for a cremation didn't amount to murder. If what my analyst said was true—that, in therapy, the feelings are the facts—then I was killing my mother.

WHILE I waited for her ashes, I fantasized about how I might part with them, the body of water I would choose, the travel required to reach its shore.

In August 1991 I'd poured what remained from my grandmother's cremation into Long Island Sound. The plot she'd bought in Los Angeles, the one from which my mother would soon be taken, was a double-decker, its upper berth reserved for my grandmother. But I hadn't complied with her request to be buried there in the same hole. It had struck me as obscene to let the two of them continue into eternity as they had in life, frozen in their suffocating struggle for ascendancy, excluding me forever. So I'd had my grandmother cremated and asked a close friend to take me out on her boat. She read the Kaddish and I followed with an excerpt from an ancient Hindu text, the Upanishads, and then I spilled my grandmother into the waves.

But the leave-taking between my mother and me would have to be private. There was no one I wanted with us.

Many hours, I sat in my study and stared out the window, accomplishing little, at least on paper. Perhaps I was making unconscious adjustments. I took it as a sign of progress that if I didn't gain weight, I did stop losing it. For the first time in memory, I was embarrassed by being too thin, grateful for weather cold enough to require long underwear as well as jeans, long sleeves that hid my arms. Suddenly, anorexia seemed less a salvation than a protracted act of hostility. Mirrors revealed my naked body to be that of a prisoner, a woman under siege, and on days that I was too tired to enjoy exercise, I didn't flog myself around the corner to the gym. I found I was no longer committed to the micromanagement of appetite and consumption; how tedious it was.

At least once a day I found myself in the kitchen, opening the freezer to retrieve my months-old milk and hold it in my hand. The bottle was one that came with my Medela breast pump. "From mother with love," it proclaimed on its side. I tested my willingness to discard this talisman, stood over the sink, hot water running, ready to melt it away, but I always put it back.

Even though it no longer had the power to protect me from the destructive, rejecting mother I'd conjured inside myself, still the bottle with its pale contents had meaning. Like a shorn baby curl, it returned me to a time and a version of myself that I wanted to remember. The bottle had become the simple, benign keepsake I'd once believed it was, something that reminded me how happy I'd felt with a baby at my breast: proud of my motherhood, blessed and whole and not in need of fixing, exactly who I wanted to be.

At 9:00 A.M. on March 3 I was hanging my little girl's coat on a hook, one among a dozen parents and baby-sitters bending to retie a shoelace, wipe a nose, kiss a head, one last caress before a morning of nursery school. I sat in a small blue plastic chair next to my daughter's and watched as she drew one of her primitive potatolike heads balanced on what appeared to be an *H*, her signature abbreviation for limbs. She used a green crayon to fill the head with three empty circles, two hungry eyes and a mouth. It was 6:00 A.M. in California, the hour at which my mother's disinterment was scheduled to begin—early enough that no visitor would be disturbed by such a sight. I said good-bye to my child, who turned her back, the only way she knew to navigate a separation without crying. On the sidewalk, I paused outside the classroom window to watch as she continued to draw, unaware of my presence. For years to come—for all our lives together—she and I would be practicing this one thing: letting each other go.

Walking home, I pictured the frail tree near my mother's grave, how it would be dwarfed by the proximity of whatever machine was used to dig up caskets— a backhoe, I guessed, its yellow teeth biting into grass, tearing down through soil. I hadn't seen that tree for years. By now it might have grown a thick trunk and high branches. Or it might be gone, replaced by a sturdier specimen.

The black granite headstone I'd selected would be taken away, crushed and recycled into gravel perhaps. How did I feel, I kept asking myself, but I didn't have an answer. Back home, I couldn't focus enough to write, so I sorted and folded laundry, picked up dry cleaning, bundled old newspapers and tied them with twine. When the phone rang at twelve-thirty I hurried to it, answered out of breath.

"It's done," the mortician said. "The remains are on their way to the crematory. And I have the necklace. It cleaned up fine. The gold didn't, uh, deteriorate or anything."

"Thank you," I said. "Thank you for calling so promptly."

I hung up and asked myself again: how, or what, did I feel? But still I had no answer. I must be in psychic post-op, I decided, lying on my metal table, touching a wound I couldn't see. Eager to know when the radical surgery I'd elected would begin to effect a cure.

The Wednesday following my mother's disinterment was Ash Wednesday. I didn't go to mass. Preoccupied as I was with my mother's cremation, it seemed redundant, and I spent most of the day at my desk. A few times I looked in the mirror, studied my bare forehead, my face unmarked by the smudgy black cross that heralded a season of penance.

Late in the afternoon I found myself in the supermarket. With three children, we always needed something, and after I became a mother I found that shopping for food was a way to comfort myself; I loved bringing the bags home and stuffing the shelves. Was it a surrogate for nursing? I wondered as I walked down the cereal aisle. The Doors' "Light My Fire" came on over the PA system, and I began to cry. How sad it was—it didn't feel bearable—letting my mother go without having had her. How many times had I sat in her car's passenger seat, listening carefully to those same lyrics played over and over? How many times had I tried to glean significance from any song she liked enough to replay? Another clue, and then another. When I had enough of them, I would know. I would know how to woo her.

In my childhood bedroom I had a prayer taped to the wall: *God grant me the serenity to accept the things I cannot change, the courage to change the things I can, and the wisdom to know the difference.* Underneath the prayer was a pencil drawing of a lion under a setting sun. It wasn't a regal lion. Rendered in profile, it was skinny and subdued, with a mournful expression. There was no cage around it, but it was a zoo animal anyway, diminished by circumstance.

"That," my mother told me when she saw the prayer, "is for alcoholics. Take it down."

"It doesn't say it's for alcoholics."

She shrugged. "Suit yourself," she said. And so I left it where it was, over my bed. What can't I change? I'd ask myself, sitting crosslegged on the quilt with my back to the wall, but I never got the answer right.

THE ASHES arrived on Monday, March 10, and I put the carton in a closet, having decided not to open it in the house. The next morning, while the children were at school and my husband at work in Manhattan, I packed the urn, still boxed, along with a beach towel and an army knife, in my favorite knapsack, the one I'd carried when my older daughter and I had made a trip together, just the two of us.

I drove east to a beach on the north fork of Long Island, not far from our summer home. It was nearly noon when I pulled into the empty parking lot, the asphalt glazed with ice. According to a local radio station, it was 28 degrees, but I found the air outside the car less frigid than I'd expected. This was the same beach where, late one winter afternoon, I'd watched needles of ice take flight from the water's edge, so I'd braced myself for a driving wind, but there was none.

Sand and snow were frozen together into fantastic, crested drifts, and the stones and shells underfoot were so thickly rimed with ice that when I bent to pick one up I found I couldn't pry it off the shore. I stood and started walking east, pulled the sleeves of my wool sweater out from my coat cuffs and held them closed around my fingers as makeshift mittens. My gloves and my sunglasses were back home, on the table by the front door, where I'd thought I'd be sure to see and bring them.

The last veil of cirrus burned away, and sun flared off every surface, so bright that it was hard to keep my head up, hard to keep my eyes open wider than a squint. Sunglasses would have made me more comfortable, but behind dark lenses I might not have seen how white was the light, I might have missed the mauve shadows cast by rocks onto the snow.

I was headed for a cove a couple of miles east from the parking lot, past three breakwaters, but the pack was heavy, and I kept losing my footing. By the time I reached the third breakwater, a graceless wall of concrete blocks that jutted into the waves, I'd fallen several times, and I stopped to rest. I set the pack down and saw deer tracks frozen into the tide-smoothed sand. Each cloven hoof had left a heart-shaped hole. I'd jogged this stretch of sand countless times and often saw deer tracks—big, frolicking loops of them, as if the animals had come to the beach to play rather than for salt water.

Shells broke underfoot. I couldn't avoid stepping on them. Whelks, jingles, clams, and moon shells the size of tennis balls were thrown far up the beach, a few all the way to the bluff. Heaped against the breakwater were mounds of purple shells, the ones called lady's slippers, frozen together at the bottom, dry and loose on top. I nudged the tip of my boot into the frozen part, trying to crack a chunk off. They weren't pretty shells, but they had been a favorite of my mother's. She liked the name, I think.

My mother and I once walked together along a breakwater. It's the only memory I have of going for a walk with her, a walk that was just a walk rather than a passage from one store to another or through the galleries of a museum. I was twenty-one, and in a month she would be forty. In a month she'd learn she had cancer and would choose not to tell me, not until after I'd moved away, from the Pacific to the Atlantic coast. But on this August afternoon we were walking abreast along a curved, stone seawall whose iron guardrail was so pocked with rust that for long stretches the metal had crumbled away, leaving no place to put your hand. The day was overcast with gusts of wind, no sunshine, just the infrequent, solitary ray, there and just as quickly gone, like a strike of lightning. Waves hit the stones under our feet with such force that what was left of the rail posts shuddered, and spray fell on us like rain, saturating our hair and clothes.

At the end of the little path into the ocean we stopped and stared in silence at the water—green, violent, limitless. Low clouds that blurred the coastline had erased the horizon entirely, and waves appeared out of a vast and churning emptiness. We hadn't spoken since leaving the cottage, wordlessly walking our way through vacation hours that were too cold and wild for a swim, too wet for window-shopping in town. Not that we ever did talk much to each other, at least not about anything besides books or movies or the answers to a crossword puzzle. Nothing personal.

But, "See the water," my mother said now, and I looked at her face instead. She had no tan—she never did—and her eyes were on the ocean, the missing horizon. "Someday it will knock all these stones down. The breakwater will be gone."

I had no answer to this. Waves crashed over and through what was left of the guardrail, leaving foam on our pant legs and shoes. My mother and I stood together, side by side, watching as one after another swell gathered, approached, and struck. When at last she turned to leave, I followed her. Both of us stepped carefully on the slick walkway.

Many times I've revisited this scene, and many times I will return. I'll try again to hear the words my mother spoke, to hear the voice that I would recognize instantly but can no longer remember. It's impossible to know, but I think that when she spoke to me on the breakwater my mother's tone was one of relief. I'd never known her to be happy, so perhaps the idea of mortality didn't frighten her. In the end, she was telling herself, time would wash everything, and every one of us, away.

Twenty years had passed since that walk we took together. Had my mother lived, she would have been sixty. I sat on the frozen beach with her ashes in my lap and watched the surf, waves so dark they looked black, each crested with a line of white foam. Endlessly, the white lines came toward me; they merged, separated, and then vanished on the icy sand. Canada geese flew high overhead, and far below them wheeled shrieking clouds of gulls. The remote cove was prettier than this spot, and more serene, but I'd chosen it before I'd recalled our standing together at the end of the old breakwater.

The urn was packed in a cardboard box, and on top of it was an envelope bearing my name. I broke the seal and withdrew the necklace I'd wanted, a fine gold chain on which hung three charms—a crucifix, a miraculous medal of the Virgin, and a garnet heart. I was surprised by the heart. I didn't remember it, and I wondered who had given it to my mother. Or perhaps she'd bought it for herself.

The black urn was made of particleboard, which explained its surprising weight, far more than the seven pounds of ash an average human is said to yield. Its lid was held in place by four black Phillips-head screws, and I had difficulty getting it off. My fingers were clumsy from the cold, and the army knife's screwdriver wasn't the right kind. Over and over it skidded from the screw heads and off the lid. Once, it nicked the palm of my left hand. Inside the urn, I found my mother's ashes double-bagged in clear plastic and closed with a twist tie. Threaded onto the tie was a tin coin, and on it was stamped the same number that appeared on the label glued to the urn: 11564.

The ashes startled me with their color and texture. Brick red and powdery, they were nothing like those of my grandmother, which had been nearly white, with visible fragments of bone. Was this the result of embalming chemicals, of her body having been underground for so many years? Later, when I called the mortuary director to ask, he told me that embalming couldn't preserve a corpse indefinitely or even for very long. As soon as ground water penetrated a casket the body inside began to decompose. If cremation followed burial, the presence of water and dirt would affect the color of the ash; decay would change its texture. So I'd been wrong all those years. She hadn't remained in her familiar form; she hadn't been waiting.

I opened the twist tie and stirred my hand through the contents of the bag. Here my mother was, reduced to dust. I had done this to her. I had pursued her across a continent, paid to have her removed from her resting place, signed the authorization to submit her body to the incinerator's fire. Seeing my work, feeling its weight in my lap, how could I not acknowledge my fury?

The annihilating force, the *it* that stalked its prey,

hadn't been my mother after all. Perhaps the black presence that terrified me—the dybbuk—had begun as my mother, her anger and rejection that I swallowed longer ago than I could remember. But over time it collected resentments, drew them to itself like a magnet does filings, like unto like: her insult, my rancor. It all became me, or at least *mine*. My rage, ancient and vindictive, with a particular target.

It hadn't been enough to reproach and accuse my mother with the example of my nursing and the unlimited opportunities it had given me to put my child's needs before my own. All along I'd also been appeasing my anger at my mother, feeding it my milk and my flesh. For if such wrath hadn't been placated, and thus distracted from its raging, then mightn't it have broken loose, taken a hostage, harmed an innocent child? Wasn't this what I'd imagined had happened to our son after I weaned his sister? That, unable to suspect his mother harbored such hostility, he'd wandered into the path of a fury I'd failed to disarm, a frenzy of anger and guilt that had the power to make him sick and choke off his life. It was to prevent such accidents that I'd literally nursed my grudge, hidden its awful face in my breast until I could bear to look at it.

How many hours—how many years—had I squandered, parsing every memory in hopes of arriving at my most precious and tightly held conceit: that I was the cheek-turner I'd been taught to imitate? Never for one moment had I been like Christ. All those times I'd found it irresistible to cut myself—that was because blood offered a means of disguising my inability to forgive my mother, blood painted over my failure with wounds that flowed like His.

I turned my palm up to consider the place where the screwdriver had torn away a shred of skin. What satisfaction a small accident such as this one used to offer, especially a cut placed as felicitously as this, in a spot reserved for stigmata. I would have impeded its healing, picked it open, peeled away as much as I needed to guarantee a scar. I studied the scrape, trying to summon some excitement in response to the sight of my blood, but there was none. Instead it struck me as exactly the wrong place for a cut, and I hoped it wouldn't bother me while I worked the next day. I was a slow enough typist without hindrance.

I unzipped my coat pocket and took out the necklace, untangled the fine chain and held it up. A heart made of fourteen tiny garnets, an image of the Virgin caught in a circle of stars, a tiny, featureless figure of Christ on the cross: together the charms swayed back and forth, disappearing into the light they reflected, their outlines dissolved by the sun. What an astonishing thing to have shimmering before my eyes. The longer I looked, the more amazed I became. I gathered the necklace into my fist and held it tightly so I could feel its substance. Eyes were suggestible; they saw what they wanted or feared, stitched up ghosts from the window curtains, conjured a visitor when there was no one at the door. But I'd never known touch to deceive.

Nearly eighteen years before, as she lay dying in a hospital, her tongue loosened by morphine, my mother had called me to her side.

"After I'm dead," she whispered, "you're going to be very angry with me."

I held her hand and squeezed her slack fingers, but I didn't say anything. I recognized her words as a gift, but I couldn't perceive its magnitude, not at twenty-three, still so many years away from being able to own my desire for vengeance.

Rejected once, and then again, again, I'd taught

myself to smother my anguish, turned my cheek, and with every turn set tinder for a rage it had taken me this long to ignite. Even my mother's implicit request for forgiveness, her admission that when my anger arrived it would be righteous—she deserved my wrath—hadn't been enough to convince me it was safe to feel it.

I'd needed a particular set of catalysts: my son's falling ill only four months after I'd weaned my daughter; the mysterious confluence of both my internist and my analyst stepping out of their familiar characters to force me up against myself; my husband's acknowledging the value in acting out certain fantasies, even—or especially—those that are profane. The loss of any one of these might have kept me from this sparkling beach, held me at my desk this bright winter day, working doggedly under the photographs on my bookcase, among them seven of my mother, always by herself. A little girl holding tight to a gatepost, a uniformed student posing in a library, a sunbather on a chaise, a young lady dressed for a dinner date, a woman reading a book, a woman in a white picture hat. That same woman sitting alone, so alone, on a stone wall.

I looked east along the shore, a familiar landscape made strange. The unblemished whiteness, the polish of ice; could winter alone have transformed a place I knew into one for which I longed, austere and celestial? I sensed the possibility of God so seldom, found so few signs to measure against my desire for them. I tired myself out, made myself sick and tired of myself as I sifted through details, determined to find the one that God was in. Always alert to whatever beauty and order might be hidden by life's chaos, its deformities; holding my breath so that I could strain a few notes of salvation out from the clamor of experience. And yet I'd never expected to arrive at this moment. Was it time that had delivered me, enough of it having passed, enough to knock down a seawall? Was it grace? Or did chance assemble the conditions necessary for my release?

I kneeled and in my cupped hands held up a portion of the ashes. Having no other words for such an occasion, I said the Lord's Prayer, and then I replaced the remains in the bag, careful to brush the adhesive red dust from my palms so that none was lost. I pulled off my boots and my two pairs of socks and stood to take off my jeans, picked up the bag and paused for a moment, half naked and holding what was left of my mother in my arms. I willed myself to feel and remember—to possess—as much as I could of this day. Then I walked into the sea with my bag of ashes, into water so cold that my bones sang with pain. When the waves reached the middle of my thighs, enough of me immersed that I could claim to be in the sea with her, I turned the bag over and poured my mother out.

The cloud of ashes hung in the surf and swirled around me, even redder now that they were wet. I was on the protected side of the breakwater, where the waves were stilled, and the red cloud didn't disperse but sent curlicues and tendrils out into the green water. It bloomed like blood and stained my legs. I stood in its midst for as long as I could stand to, then ran out to the towel, rubbed my skin dry, and dressed.

After ten minutes, the cloud had spread up the beach, tinting the foamy edge of the water pink and washing around the legs of two gulls. Oblivious, the birds dipped their heads in and drank.

I thought of waterlogged Ophelia, and I thought of myself, newly wed and rowing with my husband on the muddy Ganges. "Do you see?" I'd said to him, pointing at the legs wound in linen, the blanched face and black hair. "Do you see the body?" I'd resisted reaching out to touch the white hem of her rags, waited for my husband to say, *Yes, I see her. I see her, too.* Because she had seemed, with her staring, colorless eyes, like an apparition, a wraith that might evaporate with the rising of the sun. I watched as she floated downstream. For as long as I could see her, I watched the woman as she traveled, thinking of course of my mother, who died three years before I married.

As a bride, I wore my husband's mother's wedding dress, grateful she'd offered it to me, knowing I was lucky to have been spared the unhappiness of shopping for one alone. Together she and I took her gown to a seamstress, who squinted and pinned and then, after we had gone, cut open the bodice and resewed its seams. A month later we returned, and I tried the dress on. With the help of both women—one whom I knew little, the other not at all—I stepped into the circle of white silk, and they pulled the sleeves up my arms; they tugged the remade bodice into place. The seamstress kneeled behind me to begin the back's lower buttons, and my husband's mother worked on the top ones.

During the Quaker meeting that celebrated our marriage, my new mother-in-law looked at me beside her firstborn son, holding his hand, wearing her dress. Then she stood to speak. She turned to all the wedding guests sitting solemn and expectant on the meetinghouse benches, and she called their attention to the fact that someone was missing on this day—the bride's mother wasn't among those who had come to rejoice. The bride's mother was dead, she continued, lest someone mistake nowhere for elsewhere, a purposeful slight. My mother-in-law didn't use so stark a word as *dead* but chose a euphemism whose meaning was clear. My husband folded my fingers more tightly into his, and the guests, most of whom had never met me, looked into their laps. Silently, everyone together contemplated this absence.

Seated beside my husband on the raised bench that faced those gathered for our wedding, I looked past all the bowed heads and out of the meetinghouse windows. Their glass panes were old, with visible ripples and tiny bubbles that sparkled when sunlight blew between the branches outside. If I moved my head, tree trunks seemed to quiver in the slanting October rays. How odd, I thought, that I wasn't crying. I tried to find a square of new glass, looked for the even surface of a replacement pane, but there were none, and it seemed marvelous to me that over the course of a century not one had broken.

Fifteen years had passed since our wedding, and in

that time I hadn't returned to the meetinghouse. I wondered if all the windows were still intact, if even now, on this winter afternoon, the clear, cold light was falling in squares onto its empty benches.

Behind me, a fall of stones and earth broke away from the bluff's eroded face and raced down to the frozen sand, clattering among the shells. A gull cried out. Another answered.

I sat on my heels at the water's pleated edge and touched the pink frills of foam.

A woman, my mother, her dress dragged by the current. Departing at last, because at last I was allowing her to go.

ACKNOWLEDGMENTS

While this book was lived, I depended on the love of my husband, Colin Harrison, the wisdom of my analyst, Janet Gibbs, the company of my friend Joan Gould. And I'm indebted, not for the first time, to my exemplary doctor, Sidney K. Stein.

I have the good fortune to work with people I both love and respect. For fourteen years my editor, Kate Medina, has gracefully steered me around my blind spots, a not inconsiderable task. Amanda Urban, my agent, has seen me through ten books—eleven if I count the one she saved me from publishing. They're both women impossible to take for granted; I can't imagine how I'd fare without their guidance and their friendship.

Thank you, Carol Schneider, for the title.

Though my mother didn't prepare me for marriage or motherhood or the job of living, she did give me a muse. My love for her preceded and has outlasted my rage. Because her purpose was to elude she continues to fascinate. She provides what a writer requires, an eternally empty vessel into which endless characters and plots, and all the longing they represent, can be poured.

ABOUT THE AUTHOR

KATHRYN HARRISON is the author of the novels *Envy*, *The Seal Wife*, *The Binding Chair*, *Poison*, *Exposure*, and *Thicker Than Water*. She has also written the memoirs *The Kiss* and *The Mother Knot*; a travel memoir, *The Road to Santiago*; a biography, *Saint Thérèsa of Lisieux*; and a collection of essays, *Seeking Rapture*. She lives in New York with her husband, the novelist Colin Harrison, and their children.

Printed in the United States
by Baker & Taylor Publisher Services